This is a fictionalised biography describing some of the key moments (so far!) in the career of Christian Pulisic.

Some of the events described in this book are based upon the author's imagination and are probably not entirely accurate representations of what actually happened.

Tales from the Pitch
Christian Pulisic
by Harry Coninx

Published in the United State of America and Canada
by Leapfrog Press
www.leapfrogpress.com

Distributed in the United States by
Consortium Book Sales and Distribution
St Paul, Minnesota 55114
www.cbsd.com

First Published in the United Kingdom by Raven Books
An imprint of Ransom Publishing Ltd.
Unit 7, Brocklands Farm, West Meon, Hampshire GU32 1JN, UK
www.ransom.co.uk

ISBN 978-1-948585-91-0
Also available as an eBook
First published in the United States 2023

Copyright © 2023 Ransom Publishing Ltd.
Text copyright © 2023 Ransom Publishing Ltd.
Cover illustration by Ben Farr © 2023 Ben Farr

All rights reserved under International and Pan-American Copyright Conventions

All rights reserved. No part of this publication may be reproduced, stored in a
retrieval system, or transmitted, in any form or by any means, electronic, mechanical,
photocopying, recording or otherwise, without the prior permission of the
publishers.

The rights of Harry Coninx to be identified as the author and of Ben Farr to be
identified as the illustrator of this Work have been asserted by them in accordance
with sections 77 and 78 of the Copyright, Design and Patents Act 1988.

TALES FROM THE PITCH

CHRISTIAN PULISIC

HARRY CONINX

Leapfrog Press
New York and London

For Evie, someone who appreciates Captain America

CONTENTS

I

CAPTAIN AMERICA

June 2021, Empower Field, Mile High, Denver, USA
CONCACAF Nations League Final, USA v Mexico

"You look nervous, Chris," Giovanni Reyna barked, poking him in the back. "You're the captain – you're supposed to inspire us."

As they stood in the tunnel, waiting to go out, Christian turned to look at Gio. The 18-year-old was currently at Borussia Dortmund, breaking all the records that Christian had set only a few years earlier.

Christian tugged nervously on his armband.

"I'm not nervous," he scoffed, trying to refocus mentally. "It's a big game. You don't get many shots at an international trophy."

"Other than two years ago," Weston McKennie grumbled.

Christian frowned and nodded. He'd forgotten about two years ago. That was when the US had met Mexico in the final of the 2019 Gold Cup. The two nations had met many times before that, but that had been Christian's first taste of a major final. And they had lost.

"Other than two years ago," he agreed. "But this is different. This is a new competition. A new set of players, right? We're ready to make history."

"As long as you're not nervous," Gio replied. "We need our Captain America firing."

There were almost 40,000 fans in the stadium, split almost equally between American and Mexican fans – all waiting to find out which nation had the better team.

The two teams had played each other plenty of times, and Christian was very familiar with the Mexican players. He watched them running past, listing the danger men in his head – Jesús Corona, Héctor Herrera, Hirving Lozano.

It was an intimidating line-up and all of the Mexican players seemed to ooze confidence.

But Christian had forgotten his own strengths. He was no longer the young kid who'd struggled to get into the squad. He was the captain.

Only a month ago, he had won the Champions League with his club Chelsea, scoring in the semi-finals against Real Madrid. He was the only player on the pitch who had done that. There was no reason for him to be feeling nervous.

Nevertheless, the game started poorly for the US. Just two minutes in, a mistake at the back allowed Corona to get the ball inside their box. His first touch was good and his second even better, as he blasted the ball into the top corner.

Mexico had the lead.

The huge Mexican following in the crowd went wild and Christian was deafened by the chants that erupted around the stadium.

He looked around at his team and found ten sets

of shell-shocked eyes staring back at him. They were waiting for their captain to inspire them.

"We've got 88 minutes to get ourselves back in this, lads!" he shouted. "Forget what just happened! The game starts again now!"

But the USA had been stunned by Mexico's opener, and 20 minutes was all it took for Mexico to double their lead. Héctor Moreno rose high above the US defence and powered a header home.

Christian could barely watch their celebrations.

Then suddenly, the USA were handed a lifeline that they barely deserved. The referee went over to the VAR screen and, a moment later, the Mexican goal was ruled out for offside.

It was still 1-0.

The American fans inside the stadium celebrated the decision as if their team had just scored a goal.

Their joy was infectious and, on the pitch, the momentum started to swing in favour of the USA. Now they had their tails up and were pushing for an equaliser.

Just a few minutes later, they got it.

Christian whipped a corner in, an outswinger, looking for the head of one of the USA's tall centre-backs. It connected with Weston McKennie, but cannoned back off the woodwork.

It only came out as far as Gio Reyna, who tapped in the rebound. The USA were level.

There was no doubt that this goal would stand, and Gio raced over to Christian to celebrate, as the rest of his team-mates raced after him.

"Let's win this now, lads!" Christian demanded. "Let's make history!"

With the scores level again, both teams continued to press. Chances fell to both sides, but neither could break the deadlock.

Christian was finding it difficult to get into the game. He had to look on as Diego Lainez, subbed on by Mexico after 78 minutes, put his team ahead only a minute later.

And Christian was an observer again when Weston McKennie dragged the USA back into it with a late equaliser.

The USA had come through the semi-finals in

dramatic fashion with a late goal, and again, a late goal kept them in the match. They weren't giving this one up easily either.

At full-time it was 2-2. Extra time was to follow.

"I'm keeping you on, Chris," Manager Gregg Berhalter told him. "The truth is, you've got more in you – and you know it too. You're our captain. You're the man. Go and prove it."

With Berhalter's words ringing in his ears, Christian made his way back onto the pitch.

The first half of extra time passed without incident, but then, with six minutes left on the clock, Christian finally got his moment.

He spun with the ball in the box, before flicking it between two Mexican defenders and running through between them. As he did so, he was challenged and bundled over.

Christian went to the floor, holding his arms out, appealing for the penalty. He was sure he'd been clipped. It *had* to be a penalty. But the referee was unmoved and waved play on.

Christian shook his head. He couldn't believe it.

Then, a moment later, the ref stopped the game and walked over to the VAR screen.

"VAR must have told him to have a look," Tyler Adams said to Christian.

It didn't take long for the ref to change his mind. The USA were given a penalty.

For the second time in the match, the technology had intervened on the side of the Americans. Now they were just one kick away from winning Christian's first-ever international trophy.

There was only one man who was ever going to take that penalty. Christian placed the ball on the spot and took a deep breath. He ignored the shouts and jeers from the Mexican fans. He ignored the chatter from the Mexican players. He even ignored the encouraging comments from his own team-mates.

He was focused on one thing. The ball.

He took a short run up, not bothering to look at the keeper. His intention was clear. He was putting this in the top corner. Even if the keeper went the right way, it was going to be out of his reach.

His intentions were clear – and his aim was true. The

ball flew into the top-right corner and, even though Guillermo Ochoa had guessed the right way, he couldn't do anything about it.

GOAL! The USA were 3-2 up, with six minutes left.

Christian ripped off his shirt, not caring about the yellow card he'd inevitably be given, whirled it around and celebrated with his team-mates.

But there was still time for late drama.

Moments later, the Mexicans had their own penalty – which was deftly palmed away by substitute keeper Ethan Horvath.

The USA had done it. They had fought tooth and nail and clawed their way to win the CONCACAF Nations League.

Christian looked around at his team, the talented young players who made up the squad. For years, people had talked about the USA as a future footballing powerhouse, but he realised that their time had now arrived. Winning CONCACAF was one thing, but the next target was the world stage.

And Christian knew that he was the man to lead them there.

2

BIG DREAMS IN 15 MINUTES

June 2004, Hershey, Pennsylvania, USA
Pulisic Family Home

"Quick!" Christian yelled, sprinting up the stairs. "The whistle's just gone!"

He headed straight for his older sister's room, knowing that she'd be in there with his mum.

"What is it, Chris?" his mum asked. "What's going on?"

"We haven't got long," Christian gasped. "Will you

come and practise in the garden with me? Luís Figo has just done the most insane skill! I need to try it!"

"We can come down in a bit," his mum smiled.

"No, you don't understand," Christian moaned. "It's half-time now. I need to watch the second half!"

Christian was in the middle of watching the Euro 2004 semi-final between Portugal and the Netherlands. There were so many players he wanted to watch, to learn skills from – and this game had many of them. Marc Overmars, Ruud van Nistelrooy, Clarence Seedorf, Portugal's Cristiano Ronaldo, Deco, and his biggest idol, Luís Figo. Christian dreamed of wearing a number 10 shirt at a big club one day, following in his hero's footsteps.

In each match, Christian would pick a skill or trick that he saw one of his heroes perform, then at half-time he would take a ball out into the back yard and practise it until the 15 minutes were up and he had to race back in to catch the rest of the game.

The problem was, he needed someone to be out there with him, throwing the ball or standing in goal. His dad was at work, and now both his mum and sister were busy.

"You could ask Bob," Christian's mum suggested.

Bob was a family friend who Christian had been watching the match with, downstairs.

"Bob!" Christian shouted, running back into the living room, where the pundits on TV were analysing the match.

"Woah, slow down, Chris!" Bob said. "What's up?"

"Do you want to practise a skill Figo just did, in the yard with me?" Christian asked.

"The little stepover and the shot that hit the post?"

"Yeah, yeah!" Christian was surprised that Bob remembered it. "Let's go!" Christian burst past Bob, grabbed the ball and ran into the back yard.

"Throw me the ball. I'll do the stepover and then curl the shot. You have to try and save it," Christian told him.

Christian couldn't move his foot over the ball as quickly as Figo, but he could still do the trick. He whipped his foot around the ball, but his shot went just wide.

"Not bad," Bob said, "but try wrapping your foot round the ball more. You'll get a bit more curl on it."

Christian had forgotten that Bob had been a football coach himself, and so his advice was always welcome.

After a few more attempts, with a couple landing in the back of the net, Bob looked at Chris.

"If I remember correctly, Chris," he said. "Figo's shot was on his left foot, wasn't it? Why are you using your right?"

"I'm right-footed."

"So is Figo," Bob grinned. "The best players can use both feet." He pointed to the other side of the yard and threw the ball to Christian again. This time, using his left foot, Christian found it much harder. He didn't have the same control or power, and the ball trickled to Bob's feet.

Christian frowned. "Another!" he shouted. "Left foot!" He wasn't going to be beaten by this.

But even after trying it a few more times, he couldn't get the hang of it.

"You'll get there. You just need to do it a few more times – but you're already improving." Bob smiled. "Now, come on," he added, walking back into the house. "The second half will be starting soon."

As they walked into the lounge, Bob pointed at the television. "Now look, we've missed all the highlights from the first half."

"Don't worry," Christian smiled. "I'll watch it again later with my dad, when he gets home."

As Christian sank onto the sofa to watch the second half, he knew he was going to get there one day.

He just *knew* it.

3
FUTSAL

June 2010, Hershey, Pennsylvania, USA

"So where shall I go?" Christian asked his dad, looking around the pitch in confusion.

"Wherever you want," his dad, Mark, replied, putting his arm around his son. "It's not all tactics and formations here."

"What do you mean? Aren't there positions in the older kids' teams?" Christian asked.

They were standing on the sideline of a small pitch, out in the middle of Pennsylvania. Christian had been playing for his team, the Pennsylvania Classics, for almost two years now. He'd been part of a tight-knit group of friends, but his speed and dribbling skill had made him stand out.

He was still only 11 years old, but he'd been shuffled up a couple of age groups and was now playing with the Under-14s. Even at this age, the team were still playing on seven-a-side pitches.

Christian had felt that he was ready to play on full-size pitches, but his dad – himself a former football player and coach – had explained why this was a bad idea.

"In South America, the kids start by playing futsal, or street football, until they're about 14 or 15," he'd told his son. "If you go on an 11-a-side pitch now, you'll be exhausted when you get the ball – and when you do get it, you'll barely get any touches. And we want to maximise as many touches of the ball as possible."

It was why his dad had set up a futsal league in Philadelphia.

He'd also been keen to expose Christian to football

all over the globe. They'd regularly watch games from the Bundesliga or La Liga.

Christian had been so impressive in his dad's futsal league that he soon dreamed of playing in Europe.

He'd been offered a summer trial with Chelsea at their Cobham training ground, and he'd then spent some time training at Barcelona's world-famous La Masia academy.

"Do you remember what I said to you about futsal?" Mark reminded him. Christian nodded.

"It's the same thing here," his dad said. "You're still learning the game, getting a feel for the ball. We want you to enjoy it. We don't want you bogged down by positioning or tactics. Not yet. Just do what comes naturally and have fun. That goes for everyone on the team as well, not just you."

"So … " Christian paused. "So I can just dribble as much as I like, and not pass?"

The tiki-taka style of "pass, pass, pass" that he'd met in Barcelona hadn't been to Christian's liking. He didn't want to cut back and pass to someone else. He wanted to dribble, to show a bit of skill, to shoot.

"Just be sensible," Mark laughed. "It's not just you out there, and everyone wants to have a good time. And, you know, sometimes a pass can be just as exciting as scoring or dribbling."

Christian frowned. He was yet to be convinced that passing was exciting. He'd watched the Barcelona team that had taken everyone by storm last year. If he was honest, he preferred it when they'd had Ronaldinho – at least then they'd been exciting.

"Hey, guys, I'm Christian," he said, introducing himself to his new team-mates.

"Yeah, hi. We know who you are," one of them replied. They all knew Christian by his reputation.

The other boys were all much taller than him, but they didn't seem worried about having a kid two years younger than them as a team-mate.

In fact, most of them were excited to be alongside him.

As the players slotted into their natural positions, Christian drifted over to the left wing, where he could cut in on his right foot.

"Find me!" Christian called, as one of his team-mates

picked up the ball. This was the only time when he liked passing – when they were passing to him.

The ball was fizzed over to Christian and he controlled it delicately with the inside of his right foot. Two opposition players surrounded him, seeing an easy opportunity to take the ball off the small kid.

But Christian effortlessly skipped between them, before stepping over the ball, just as he'd learned from Luís Figo, and fired a shot towards goal.

It flew over the bar.

"There was a pass on there, Chris!" his coach called. But then he added, "Nice dribbling though!"

From then on, Christian was given more space on the pitch, as the opposition grew wary of the little kid with the quick feet.

He found the net a couple of times, and even allowed himself to pass to his team-mates every now and then. He didn't want to be accused of being selfish, even if it was annoying each time he gave the ball to someone else.

"Amazing job today, Chris. Well done!" his dad said, as he walked off the pitch.

"Let's get going," Christian replied. "The World Cup matches will be on soon."

"Keep playing like that and you'll be there yourself soon!" his coach laughed. "Thought you might be hungry," he added, as he threw a pack of Doritos Christian's way.

Christian glanced at his dad. "Am I allowed these?" He knew that he'd need to drink and eat healthily if he wanted to make it to the top.

"Course you are!" Mark laughed. "After those skills, I'd say you've earned them. Maybe save some to watch the World Cup with, though!"

Christian grinned and ripped the bag open. Some people at Chelsea and Barcelona's academies had told him it was impossible to become a top player growing up in the USA. They said you had to go to Europe.

But he was loving life in Pennsylvania.

In fact, he couldn't see why he'd ever leave.

4
THE TOUR

February 2015, Strobelallee Training Centre,
Dortmund, Germany

"So, what's it going to take to get you here at Dortmund?" the club's Sporting Director, Michael Zorc, asked Christian and his dad.

Christian had never really intended to come to Europe, but after he'd started training with the older teams, it had quickly become clear that he was playing well above and beyond the level of the Pennsylvania Classics.

Mark knew a scout in professional football, who'd offered to help them work out which was the best club for Christian to join. His list of clubs included some from the Premier League, the Bundesliga and La Liga.

Mark had arranged a meeting with the scout.

"I hope he suggests Barcelona," Mark said before the meeting. "You enjoyed your time at La Masia, didn't you, Chris?"

Barcelona had a history of bringing players like Lionel Messi, Xavi and Andrés Iniesta through their academy, but Christian wasn't sure about a team that prioritised passing so much.

"I want to play for a more direct, attacking team than Barca," Christian said, as they walked into the meeting room.

"Then I have the perfect team to recommend to you," the scout interruputed with a smile, as he stood to greet father and son.

It turned out that the scout knew all the European clubs well. And he was clear in his recommendation. Not Barcelona. Not the Premier League and all its money. The answer was obvious.

"If you want to develop into a top player, Christian, you shouldn't go to England or Spain. You should go to Germany."

Christian and his dad looked at each other, eyebrows raised.

"I've sent some clips of you to a few clubs, and one of the biggest teams in the country, with one of the best academies, wants to talk to you. Borussia Dortmund."

"Seriously?" Christian smiled.

He'd watched Jürgen Klopp's Dortmund win the Bundesliga and reach the Champions League final a few years ago. They played fast, attacking football that Christian knew would suit him.

Mario Götze and Robert Lewandowski had left, but this was still a Dortmund team that contained Marco Reus, Henrikh Mkhitaryan and Pierre-Emerick Aubameyang.

"They're willing to fly you out to Germany to talk to you and let you have a look at their facilities," the scout continued. "What do you think?"

"Can we go today?" Christian asked his dad excitedly.

"Hold your horses, mate," Mark laughed. "You can't

assume they'll want to sign you. And even if they do, we'll need to make sure they're the right fit."

A few days later, Christian was delighted to miss a few days of school to fly to Dortmund with his dad.

They were given a tour of the training ground and introduced to members of the staff. Then something happened that Christian wasn't ready for.

"Hey! Christian, isn't it?" He turned around to see who had called his name. And suddenly, there was Jürgen Klopp, standing in front of him.

"Er, yeah," Christian replied nervously.

"I hope you like what you see around here. I'll be seeing you soon, eh? Good lad," Klopp said, putting his hand on Christian's shoulder, before walking off to lead first-team training.

And now they were sitting in a Dortmund meeting room, across the table from the club's Sporting Director, Michael Zorc. This was the final stage of negotiations.

"Everything looks great," Christian's dad said. "But we've got plenty of options here. What makes Dortmund the right choice for Christian? Why shouldn't we go over to La Masia, for example?"

"We know what type of player Christian is," Zorc replied, gesturing over to him. "He fits our style of play perfectly."

He paused for a moment. "We've got a great reputation for developing youngsters here at Dortmund. We don't *buy* superstars, we *make* them. You know we're not going to buy a new winger to block Christian's path to the first team. We'll give him the time he needs to develop."

He paused again and looked at Christian. "And look, if you want to go to Barcelona in a few years' time, we can make sure you're ready to make an impact there."

It was a convincing argument and Christian turned to his dad, a pleading look in his eyes. He wanted to join the club.

"There's one more thing," Mark said. "Christian has only got an American passport, so he won't be able to come here until he's 18, in two years' time."

Michael smiled. "My sources tell me your grandad is Croatian, right?" he asked Christian. "So we can get you an EU passport, and you'll be able start training with us immediately."

"Well it looks like you've got everything covered," Christian's dad admitted.

Christian had never seen his dad look so impressed. That was when he knew that this was it. He was going to be a Dortmund player.

He was taking the first step on his journey to become a professional footballer – with a new club, and in a new country.

5
DEBUT

January 2016, Signal Iduna Park, Dortmund, Germany
Borussia Dortmund v Ingolstadt

"You sure you're old enough to be sitting here?" Erik Durm grinned, as he squeezed onto Dortmund's bench, next to Christian.

"Age is only a number," Christian smiled.

"You're too smart for your own good," Erik replied, shaking his head.

Seventeen years, four months and 12 days. That's

how old Christian was, sitting there for the first time on the Dortmund bench. He knew, because his dad had told him so before the game. Mark wasn't going to let Christian forget it.

It had been a frustrating start to Christian's time in Germany. He'd been at Dortmund for almost a year now, but was yet to make an appearance in their starting eleven.

He didn't speak German very well, and he didn't have any friends or family with him, which made it even harder.

There were some parts of "America" that Christian could enjoy in Germany, like Chipotle, the chain of Mexican food restaurants that gave him a taste of home. On the pitch, Mexico might have been the USA's biggest rivals, but Christian loved Mexican food and was willing to travel two hours from his home in Dortmund to get it.

"At school, I can't even tell if I'm in a math or a science class," he told his mum on the phone, as he devoured a burrito. "That's how good my German is. You know, maybe I should just have gone to an MLS club."

"You can come home any time you want, Christian," his mum told him reassuringly. "But I thought you wanted to reach the top? You've known all along that you couldn't do that if you stayed here."

He knew she was right. Wanting to be the best player he could possibly be was the one thing to keep him going.

The big problem had been the delay in getting him his EU passport. Without it, he couldn't play in any formal games – which just left him training with the U-17s or the U-19s.

But things had turned a corner at the end of last season. There had been upheaval when Jürgen Klopp departed, after nearly 10 years as manager, but, for Christian, there had been only good news.

He'd finally got his passport, so was allowed to play matches for the youth teams. He was now playing regularly at weekends – and he was scoring goals.

Christian had never been a prolific scorer back in the US. He was a dribbler, a skilful player who would run past defenders. He liked to shoot, of course, but he was never that successful. After dribbling past so many opposition players, he often found himself too exhausted to get a lot of power behind any shot.

But now, even before the winter break, he'd scored 10 goals in just 15 games.

It had prompted a quick decision from Thomas Tuchel, the new Dortmund boss.

"I know you're only 17, Chris, but I can't ignore the goals you're scoring. From now on, you're training with the first team," he told the youngster.

"Wait, really?"

"You don't think you're ready?"

"No, no! I do. It's just a surprise."

"I'll get some of the lads to introduce themselves to you. You'll get settled in no time."

"Here's the next big thing!" Marco Reus announced with a grin, as Christian walked onto the first-team training pitch for the first time. The American shyly bowed his head.

"Don't be afraid of any of these guys – just do your thing," Marco told him, putting his arm around him.

"Don't worry," Christian smiled, "I've been playing with guys older than me all my life."

And now, today, it was the real deal. He was starting on the bench, but it was a real Bundesliga game – against Ingolstadt. This was what he'd been desperate to be involved in.

If he got on today, he'd be the eighth youngest player ever – *and* by far the youngest American – to play in the Bundesliga.

His dad had been even more excited than Christian. It was Mark Pulisic who had looked up all the records and who'd made sure that friends and colleagues back home in Pennsylvania would be watching the game live.

"It'll be like eight in the morning over there!" Christian laughed. "And I might not even get on!"

"It doesn't matter, Chris," his dad insisted. "Most of them watched you as a kid. They're excited. They want to support you!"

The game didn't go as well as anyone in black and yellow had hoped. With just 20 minutes left, it was still 0-0, and Christian didn't see any way he was going to get on.

But he was the one who got the nod. There was nobody else on the bench that Tuchel could turn to.

"Christian, get your tracksuit off! You're coming on!" he suddenly heard Tuchel shout. The rain was pouring down, but he'd never taken a tracksuit off more quickly in his life.

"You're the best attacker I've got to bring on," the manager told him. "Just work super-hard, get stuck in. Try something different. We're open to all ideas."

Christian suddenly realised that, with the fans' support, he wasn't alone in Germany.

He wanted to remember this moment – his professional debut – for the rest of his life. He needed to savour every little detail.

But in a flash, it was all over. Aubameyang's two late goals sealed a 2-0 win for Dortmund, and, even though Christian had barely been involved, it didn't matter.

He was now officially a professional footballer.

6
CALL-UP

March 2016, Mapfre Stadium, Columbus, Ohio, USA
World Cup Qualifiers, USA v Guatemala

"The boss is calling for you," one of the coaches called over to Christian, as he sat eating his lunch.

"What do you mean? He's here," Christian said, looking across at Thomas Tuchel, sitting opposite him in the canteen at Dortmund's training ground.

"No, not him. The America boss. Klinsmann. He's on the phone in the office."

The coach was being so casual about it, but his words had shaken Christian. Jürgen Klinsmann, the USA national team coach, was on the phone. For him.

Did that mean what he thought it meant? Was he about to be called up for the World Cup Qualifiers? Aged just 17?

Leaving his lunch, Christian raced into the training building and ran upstairs into the office. He answered the phone breathlessly, trying to gather himself.

"Hello?" he asked cautiously, trying to mask the excitement in his voice.

"Hello, is that Christian?"

"Yes," he said, his voice catching in his throat. "Yes, it is."

"Great. This is Jürgen Klinsmann, the US coach."

"I know who you are. I can recognise you by your accent."

"Ha ha! That's good. Yes. Well, look, I'm just phoning to let you know that I want you in the squad for the match against Guatemala. Are you OK with that?"

"Oh, right … yes, great, thanks … " Christian replied, not sure what to say.

"OK, good. That's good. Ah – see you soon, then," was all Jürgen said, before ending the call.

Christian didn't know what to do with himself as he put the phone down. The first person he told was his dad, who was predictably ecstatic – repeatedly telling Christian how proud he was.

"Have I made the right decision?" Christian asked, when his dad had calmed down.

Christian was talking about choosing to play for the USA instead of for Croatia, which he could have done because of his grandad.

"Well, you were born and raised in the US. The team can grow with you."

"Yeah, I think you're right," Christian replied.

"If you get on the pitch, you'll be the youngest player for the USA in a World Cup qualifier," his dad continued. "Imagine if you score!"

"I'm just happy to be part of the squad," Christian insisted.

The game was being played in Columbus, Ohio, four hundred miles from Christian's family home.

"It's funny how I'm so used to Dortmund now that

it feels weird being back in the US," Christian told his mum on the morning of the match. Somehow, Germany now felt more like home.

As the players walked out of the dressing room, Christian found himself surrounded by American soccer legends – players like Clint Dempsey, Jozy Altidore and Michael Bradley.

"I think you might be half my age," legendary goalkeeper Tim Howard said, with a shake of his head. "But welcome aboard, anyway! You younger guys are the future of this team."

"I'm just here to learn from the best," Christian replied with an awed smile.

As expected, he started on the bench, but after 50 minutes, USA were 3-0 up and cruising. Minutes later, he heard Klinsmann calling to him.

"Go and warm up, Christian!"

He pulled on his training top and jogged along the touchline, breaking into a few stretches to get his muscles going. He could feel the eyes of the stadium on him. *Who was this 17-year-old? Who did he play for? Where had he come from?*

The Dortmund stadium may have been louder, with a better atmosphere, but, for an American, this was something else. It didn't get any better than this.

With 10 minutes left, Klinsmann called Christian back from his warm-up.

"OK. You're ready, Chris," he said. "Trust me, you're ready. Just keep doing what you've been doing for Dortmund for the last few months. You'll be fine."

Once more, as he ran out onto the pitch, he tried to remember everything, to savour the moment – a moment that would stay with him for the rest of his life.

Christian didn't have many chances to show his quality in his short time on the pitch, but it didn't matter. Now, at just 17 years of age, he was an American international.

He was in the history books.

7

TWO IN TWO

April 2016, Mercedes-Benz Arena, Stuttgart, Germany
Stuttgart v Borussia Dortmund

"You've got to be on your toes, Chris," Pierre-Emerick Aubameyang explained, gesturing with his hands.

After almost a month out of the Dortmund first team, Christian had made cameo appearances against Liverpool in the Europa League and Werder Bremen and Schalke at home.

But he was still searching for that elusive first goal.

Which was why he was now talking to Aubameyang. The Gabonese striker had scored 25 goals last season and was already past that tally this year. He was Dortmund's most prolific striker – if anyone knew about scoring goals, it was him.

"You have to be ready, Chris," Aubameyang repeated, a big grin on his face. "If Mhiki has a shot, you expect the rebound. If Marco is lining up a cross, you should already be in the box."

"Won't the defender be doing the same thing?" Christian asked. "Shouldn't I be practising shooting?"

"Practise?" Aubameyang laughed loudly. "You can practise for hours and hours, but it won't prepare you for the real thing. Shooting is luck. It bounces and bobbles. You just get power and you'll do fine."

"And the defender?"

"You have to be smarter than the defender," Auba insisted. "This is what I'm telling you. You need to be in position *before* the defender has even realised what's happening. Take a risk. It won't always come your way. But when it does … "

He paused, leaving it unspoken.

Christian understood what Aubameyang was telling him.

The next game was at home against Hamburg, a team well down the table. There wasn't a lot at stake at this stage of the season, so Tuchel was happy to mix it up and give more players a chance.

"You'll be starting against Hamburg," Tuchel told Christian a few days before the match. "I know you're itching to score your first goal, but just relax and it'll come."

Christian got his chance early. Dortmund worked the ball into the box and Mats Hummels flicked it into Christian's path. He got it onto his right foot, opening his body up and sticking an arm out to hold off the defender's challenge.

He remembered Auba's words. "Just go for power."

He struck it as hard as he could. It whistled across the ground and through the arms of the keeper, landing in the back of the net.

GOAL!

He'd done it. He had his first professional goal.

"I'm glad I was the one to give you the assist on your

first goal," Hummels told him during the celebrations. "When you've scored a few hundred, my name will be in the history books too!" he laughed.

"Don't get ahead of yourself, mate!" Christian grinned.

Aubameyang wasn't satisfied though.

"Two in two," he kept telling Christian the following week, every time he came across him on the training ground. "Let's make it two in two."

The next game was away at Stuttgart and, once more, Christian found himself in the starting line-up, joining the likes of Marco Reus, Henrikh Mkhitaryan and Shinji Kagawa in midfield.

Kagawa opened the scoring in the first half, giving Dortmund the lead. Then, just before half-time, Mkhitaryan got the ball on the edge of the box and opened his body up as if he was going to shoot.

Recalling Aubameyang's advice, Christian was already on the move. That gave Mhiki the option to slip a pass into him – or at least it put him in the best position if the shot was saved.

Mkhitaryan blasted the ball towards goal and it was

blocked by the keeper, but the ball squirmed away from him and came back out. It fell right at Christian's feet.

He couldn't believe his luck. The defenders hadn't reacted in time and now he was barely six yards from goal, with the keeper already on the floor. He struck it first time with his left foot. The keeper got a glove to it, but it wasn't enough.

GOAL!

Christian had his two in two.

He celebrated even more wildly this time.

"I could get used to this," Christian laughed to Aubameyang.

"It never gets old!" the goal-machine striker replied.

Christian had cemented his place in the history books but, more importantly, he'd established himself in the Dortmund first team and planted his name in the minds of scouts and pundits around the world.

He was no longer just a skilful dribbler with high potential.

Now, he was a goal-scorer.

8
UP AND DOWN

September 2016, Arnos Vale Playing Ground, St Vincent and the Grenadines, St Vincent and the Grenadines v USA

"Hey, are you Christian Pulisic?" a teenage girl shouted across the street, as Christian walked down Hershey's main street. "Can I have a picture?"

Christian still wasn't used to being recognised in public.

Even though football wasn't the most popular sport in the USA, he'd become a household name – the man who was going to lead the US national team to world glory.

Many players who'd been tipped to do the same had come and gone. Now, it was Christian's turn. His Dortmund team-mates had given him the nickname "Captain America" – and it had been picked up by the American press.

There were even calls from some quarters for Klinsmann to give still-17-year-old Christian the captaincy now.

He'd scored his first goal for his country in a friendly against Bolivia, prior to the Copa América tournament over the summer. And he'd spent his evenings looking at the messages and comments flooding social media.

Get Pulisic in the starting line-up.

This boy has got something special.

Pulisic is unreal.

He'd felt the pressure at Dortmund, with the eyes of the club's 60,000 fans on him. But now there were 300 million Americans watching his every move. Every pass, every flick, every touch was scrutinised. It was way more than he'd ever experienced before.

But his dad had seen it coming and, for years, he'd been preparing Christian for the limelight.

"You can't control what everyone says about you," Christian remembered Mark telling him, back in the days of Pennsylvania Classics. "Just focus your attention on what you *can* control and don't worry about anything else."

The tournament was a success for the USA and they went all the way to the semi-finals. But, for Christian, it was a personal disappointment. He barely played, and when he did play, he struggled. It didn't go unnoticed by the press and the fans that the US had lost every tournament game he'd been involved in.

Once more, he found himself glued to his phone, watching the messages come through.

Pulisic starting to believe his own hype #overrated

We lost every game Pulisic played ... I thought he was supposed to be good

So much for Captain America. More like Captain LOSER!

It was almost a relief when the international break was over and Christian could return to the relative safety of Germany. He had never thought he'd be keen to get away from the USA – he'd always felt comfortable there. But now it had become too much.

So, when the next World Cup qualifiers came around, it was almost a disappointment that he was part of the team. He didn't want the scrutiny, the pressure.

"How do you handle it?" he asked Jozy Altidore, another who'd been dubbed the saviour of American football.

"Just ignore it. Delete all the social media apps from your phone."

"No way!"

"Then use it," Jozy offered. "Use the negative comments to prove them wrong. Or prove them right. Whatever you need to do. Just use it to get you going. Get you fired up."

USA's first World Cup qualifier was against St Vincent and the Grenadines. Christian started on the bench, but with 20 minutes left he was brought on.

Time to show everyone what I'm really made of, he thought, as he jogged onto the pitch.

It didn't take long.

A free-flowing move from the US found the feet of

Sacha Kljestan. Christian was already on the move on the other side of the box.

"Sacha!" he bellowed, sticking an arm in the air.

The ball was floated into him. His first touch controlled it perfectly, taking him clear of the defender. His second slotted the ball in the back of the net.

GOAL!

He'd become the youngest person to score for the United States in a World Cup qualifier.

Moments later, Christian returned the favour, bursting clear into the box and rolling it back for Kljestan to tap home.

"A goal and assist in less than five minutes is pretty good going!" Sacha said to Christian.

There was still time for more, though.

In added time, the ball was cut back to Christian. He was on the edge of the box and under some pressure. He got it onto his right foot and curled it towards goal.

The keeper didn't even move as the ball settled in the back of the net. Christian had scored twice.

He raised his arms, celebrating the goal, knowing

that he'd added himself to the history books once more. He also knew that he'd proved a lot of people wrong.

As soon as he got in the dressing room, he was on his phone, scrolling through social media, looking for comments and critiques. He was going to do what Jozy had told him.

He was going to use it.

9
FIRST TROPHY

May 2017, Olympiastadion, Berlin, Germany
DFB-Pokal Final, Borussia Dortmund v Eintracht Frankfurt

"I just don't know where I fit in," Christian told his dad. "I thought I was going to play more this season, but it's not happening."

When Christian had joined Dortmund, he'd been told by Michael Zorc that they didn't sign superstars – they made them. So, after signing a new contract in January that would keep him at the club until 2020, he was surprised and disappointed when several players who played in his position were signed over the summer. This included Mario Götze, Ousmane Dembélé and André Schürrle.

"I guess I was hoping to play 30-plus games this year," Christian admitted. "Maybe hit ten goals."

Mark laughed before replying. Christian had always been the ambitious one in the family, leading his own quest for self-improvement, demanding extra practice and wanting to play football every waking minute.

"You might want to lower your expectations, Chris. You're not even 18 yet! Most players haven't even reached the first team until their twenties."

"I don't want to be *most players*. I don't want to be *another guy* full of potential. I want to push on, make it happen."

"The best person to talk to is Tuchel," Mark replied. "Let him know what you're thinking. It's the only way you can get everything sorted in your own mind."

Christian wasn't sure. Tuchel had always been good to him – his door was always open and he was the one who'd got Christian into the first team.

But he'd seen Tuchel's other side too. He wasn't someone who suffered fools easily. If he disagreed with what you said, then you'd know it. Maybe for now it was better just to keep his head down.

It didn't take long for it to become clear that Tuchel wasn't going to cast Christian aside just yet. After sitting on the bench for the first two games, he was thrust into the starting eleven against Darmstadt.

He rewarded his manager with a goal and two assists.

For the rest of the season, Christian was used sparingly, often playing 20 minutes or so from the bench.

"I want you to use your pace and skills to overwhelm tired defenders," Tuchel told him. "At your age, your body is still developing, so we can't expect you to play the full 90 minutes with the intensity that we need."

Christian found his lack of time on the pitch frustrating, but a conversation with former Dortmund star Mario Götze reminded him why it was important.

"I burst onto the scene at 18 as well," Götze admitted. "I played 40 games a year, got my dream move to Bayern. I even scored the winner in the World Cup final."

"You're talking as if that's a bad thing. It sounds like a dream career to me," Christian laughed.

"I played too much," Götze said bluntly. "The pressure, all that game time. I've got so many injury problems now – more than most players my age. You've got to be careful, Chris. The boss is doing the right thing, easing you in."

So Christian developed his style of play to become the ultimate impact sub. He could come on and influence a game in the space of 10 minutes. The key moments began adding up. An assist against Real Madrid in the Champions League, a goal and an assist against Leverkusen.

When he was named on the bench for the final game of the season, the DFB-Pokal final against Eintracht Frankfurt, Christian wasn't worried. He knew that he would get a chance to get on.

He watched the first half eagerly from the bench. Ousmane Dembélé fired Dortmund into the lead, before Ante Rebic´ pulled Frankfurt level.

Then, moments before half-time, Marco Reus pulled up injured. Christian was the man to replace him.

"Do what you've been doing all season, Chris," Tuchel told him. "Work hard, dribble, shoot. Don't be afraid."

Both sides got their share of chances. Frankfurt hit the post. Aubameyang had a shot cleared on the line. Then, just 20 minutes into the second half, Christian got his chance.

The ball was floated into the box, where Christian had already made a typical darting run. He got ahead of the defenders and got to the ball first, just as the keeper was charging out. As the ball bounced, Christian stuck out a leg and got the first touch.

The ball rolled past the keeper and Christian went to go with it, but the keeper clattered into Christian, knocking him to the floor. He tumbled over, watching the ball roll out of play.

"Penalty!" the Dortmund players all yelled.

It had to be, surely. The referee agreed and pointed to the spot.

Moments later, Aubameyang had scored and Dortmund were 2-1 up.

The next 25 minutes passed in a flash and, before

he knew it, Christian was putting a DFB-Pokal Cup-winners medal around his neck.

"How does it feel?" Shinji Kagawa asked him, just after he'd lifted the trophy.

"Like I'm on top of the world!"

It was Christian's first major honour and Dortmund's first trophy in five years – and he'd played a key role. He'd won the penalty that had won them the game.

His second season at Dortmund had topped his first. He'd played 43 games and been directly involved in 18 goals. And to cap it all, he had won his first silverware.

He couldn't wait for next year to begin.

10
QUESTIONS

August 2017, Signal Iduna Park, Dortmund, Germany
German Super Cup, Borussia Dortmund v Bayern Munich

"Hard pressing," Peter Bosz told the players in the dressing room. "That's the Dortmund way, and that's my way. We win the ball back quickly, far up the pitch and in high numbers."

He paused, looking around at the tense faces before him. "We won a final at the end of last season. Now let's start this season by winning another!"

Dortmund's DFB-Pokal success had landed them in a second cup final. The Super Cup, between the Bundesliga champions and the DFB-Pokal Cup winners, was always played at the beginning of a new season.

This game pitted Dortmund against arch-rivals Bayern Munich, the dominant team in the country – a team that Dortmund had been trying to topple for years.

There had once more been a significant summer change at the club. Thomas Tuchel, the man who had shown so much faith in Christian and who had given him his opportunity in the first team, had gone.

He had been replaced by the Dutch coach Peter Bosz, who Dortmund had bought out from his Ajax contract for a record fee.

Nevertheless Bosz was an unknown quantity, and so the Super Cup final took on new meaning for the Dortmund players. Now, it became an opportunity to impress the new manager.

Bosz was a more attacking coach than Tuchel had been and there was a greater emphasis on scoring goals – something which suited Christian down to the ground.

He was an attacking player at heart and he knew that one of the things Tuchel had been keen to instil in him was more defensive discipline.

It was obvious to Christian that the new manager could see something in him, so he wasn't too surprised to be given a place in the starting line-up for the final.

He completed a vibrant front three, alongside Pierre-Emerick Aubameyang and Ousmane Dembélé.

"I want direct passes into our forward players," Bosz told the team. "Get the ball forward quickly and play with urgency. They're not the quickest back there. We can overwhelm them."

"Chris, they'll try and play out from the back," Bosz told him. "But they're not always the best. If we can pressure early, get in amongst them, we can win the ball back and cause problems. There will be chances."

It was supposedly a final with no "home" or "away" teams, but the match was being played in Dortmund's stadium and, as Christian came out onto the pitch, he could see that there were far more Dortmund fans. The "yellow wall" was in full voice. In fact, he could barely see any Bayern fans in the ground.

For Christian it felt like just yesterday that he'd been playing in his last cup final.

The game began sluggishly, neither team playing with much urgency. Both teams were still finding their fitness after the summer break, but for Dortmund – and Christian in particular – there was a new boss to impress. A slow start wasn't going to cut it.

Bayern went to play across the back, but a touch by Javi Martinez was slightly heavy. Christian was ready.

He was the first there, nipping the ball off the toes of the Bayern centre-back and shrugging off his challenge. The other defenders were too far away to make a difference – he knew they wouldn't catch him.

It was just him and the keeper now. He took a few touches, settling his nerves and feeling the ball at his feet. The keeper came out, making himself big. Christian looked at him, not looking at the ball or the goal.

He didn't want the keeper to know where he was going. He opened his body up and feinted, as if he was going to sweep it into the near corner, but instead slid it past the keeper and into the far corner. It rolled past him and settled in the back of the net.

GOAL!

Christian turned and sprinted towards the fans, arms aloft. He had scored on the opening day of the season, in the Super Cup final, against Bayern Munich.

At just 18.

"I don't think I've ever seen a better start to the season for an eighteen-year-old," Aubameyang said to Christian as they celebrated.

This was the biggest moment of his career so far, topping everything that had gone before, including his games and goals for the USA.

Now they just needed to hold on.

Bosz's new style of play brought chances and goals, but it also left the defence vulnerable, and Lewandowski soon pulled a goal back for Bayern. Aubameyang chipped Dortmund back in front, but then a scrambled own goal made it 2-2.

With the game heading to penalties and Christian exhausted, he was subbed off. He had done his part and his clinical finish had impressed the new manager in the process.

It wasn't the end to the game that he'd wanted, but

as Christian collapsed in his seat, he knew it was the right call. There was no way he could have taken a penalty.

Instead, he watched as Bayern were the more ruthless team. They won the shootout 5-4 and it was Bayern who went on to lift the Super Cup.

Dortmund had been attacking, hard pressing, brilliant going forward – but they'd fallen short.

For the first time in his young career, Christian began to wonder about being at Dortmund. There was so much change at the club every summer, and they didn't seem to be getting any closer to Bayern.

Was it the right place for him to continue his career?

II
OUT

October 2017, Ato Boldon Stadium, Couva, Trinidad
World Cup Qualifiers, Trinidad and Tobago v USA

"We can't play on this, surely!" Bobby Wood exclaimed to Christian and the rest of the US squad, as they warmed up.

Christian pressed his boot down into the ground and it made a soft squelching sound, as the waterlogged pitch sank beneath his studs. Half of his boot disappeared in the muddy water.

He passed a ball towards Bobby, but it instantly stopped as soon as it hit a puddle.

"There's nothing we can do," the manager, Bruce Arena, said, marching over to the team. "Remember, they'll be playing on the same pitch as us. We've just got to carry on."

The "they" in question were Trinidad and Tobago, the USA's opposition for today's match – the final match of World Cup qualifying.

Christian had been in good form so far in the qualifiers, with six goals to his name. He'd even scored twice against today's opponents in the home game.

But, today's game was the most important match of the campaign so far. This was the match that could qualify the USA for the 2018 World Cup in Russia.

A poor start to qualifying had cost Jürgen Klinsmann his job and he'd been replaced by the current boss, Bruce Arena. He had steadied the ship somewhat and, with one match to go, the USA were in a good position to qualify.

Christian didn't follow the stats himself, but he'd spoken to his dad the previous night.

"If we win or draw, we qualify," Mark had told his son. "If we lose, and Honduras and Panama also lose, we still qualify. If one of them loses and we lose, we still go into the play-offs. And they're playing Mexico and Costa Rica – we're playing bottom-of-the-table Trinidad."

"Well, as far as I'm concerned, we've got to win," Christian insisted. "We don't want to ride our luck, having to rely on other people."

"Of course," his dad replied. "But the stats say we've got a 90% chance of progressing."

Christian agreed, but something didn't feel right with him. There was a lot of talk in the squad and in the media, as if qualification was a done deal.

Maybe it was the thunderstorm the night before that had flooded the pitch. Maybe it was the fact that he'd seen several members of the Trinidadian squad talking about 1989, when the US had stopped them from qualifying.

Whatever. He just had a bad feeling about the game.

Even training had been difficult. The US squad had needed to cross a small river to get to their training ground, after the rains had besieged the island. And today the pitch wasn't doing them any favours.

Nevertheless, carrying the dreams of what the World Cup would hold for their team, the US fans in attendance were in an excited mood as the players walked onto the pitch.

Christian had barely had time to adjust to the weather and the pitch, when the game began. He didn't feel ready at all. And neither, it seemed, did the rest of the team.

After just 17 minutes, Trinidad and Tobago broke the deadlock. A cross was swept in from the right-hand side and, as Omar Gonzalez went to clear, he hooked the ball over his head, over the head of keeper Tim Howard and into the back of the net.

Just like that, the US were one down.

Christian frowned and shook his head. He went searching for the ball, trying to drag his team back into the game, but the US players were shell-shocked. Every pass went astray, every shot went wide.

Not long after, Trinidad doubled their lead. A booming strike from Alvin Jones, 35 yards from goal, twisted and turned in the air and snaked past Tim Howard.

2-0.

Now Christian knew that, unless the US turned things around quickly, they were in real trouble. They'd have to rely on results elsewhere going their way, to reach the World Cup.

Every few minutes, Christian would turn towards the sidelines, seeking out a coach to find the scores from the other games. As far as he could tell, Costa Rica and Mexico were still winning, meaning that the USA were still going to the World Cup.

At half-time, that was still where things stood. Unsurprisingly, the manager wasn't happy.

"I don't care about the weather, boys," he growled. "This isn't good enough. We go out there and we turn it around. Show me you deserve to be in this team. Show me you deserve to be at the World Cup. 'Cos right now … none of you do."

The team clapped and cheered to fire themselves up. Christian looked around the dressing room and suddenly he could see a flame in their eyes that hadn't been there before.

Experienced forward Clint Dempsey was subbed on

at half-time to give the team some direction, and he made an instant impact, pushing the Americans up the pitch.

Just 80 seconds into the second half, they got a goal back.

The ball was flicked into Christian on the edge of the box. He shifted it onto his right foot and whipped an effort towards goal. It sailed between a crowd of players and evaded the dive of the keeper, landing in the back of the net.

Christian pumped his fist, celebrating his goal, but he kept it muted. They were still losing. He could hear the pocket of American fans going wild in the stadium. He wanted to win this for them.

Urged on by the fans, the US kept pushing. Dempsey had a shot saved, and then another hit the post. Jozy Altidore went close and Omar Gonzalez headed over. It was a different American side from the first half, but still they remained 2-1 down. Trinidad were defending with everything they had.

Christian turned to the sidelines, hoping to hear some positive news about the other games, but it wasn't good. Panama and Honduras had both turned things around. As it stood, the USA were going out.

The news inspired another wave of US attacks as they desperately pushed for the goal that could save them. But it never came. Trinidad and Tobago wanted revenge – and they got it.

As the final whistle blew, Christian collapsed to his knees. He'd left everything on the pitch to try to drag the US to the World Cup, but it hadn't been enough. The media and the fans would be savage in their reaction, but nobody was as harsh a critic as Christian himself. He felt he had let his country down.

"Captain America" Pulisic was supposed to be the man to lead the US team to new heights, but instead their 24-year run at World Cups had come to an end.

"You couldn't have done anything more, mate," his team-mates said, as they lifted Christian to his feet.

"As long as I'm in the team, this is never going to happen again," he replied, shaking his head.

"I've let my country down," he told his dad later that day, when they met up in the hotel.

"I think it's more that *they* let *you* down! You were

having to do everything out there," Mark replied. "I know they're saying it's the most humiliating loss in the national team's history, but that's not on you, Chris. You've got to look foward now. You've got time to turn this around."

His dad was right. Christian vowed he would *never* let this happen again.

No matter what, he would get the USA to the World Cup next time.

No. Matter. What.

12
A NEW CHALLENGE

January 2019, Christian's House, Dortmund, Germany

"Chelsea, Arsenal or Liverpool?" That was the question that Christian's dad had asked him over the winter of 2018.

Just as in the previous two seasons, Christian's third season in Dortmund's first-team squad had been mixed.

It had been another season of changes, with a couple

of different managers, and Christian had struggled to find consistency.

But this year, he'd been more impressive. He was becoming a talisman for club and country, and that had attracted plenty of interest from clubs all around Europe.

He'd even finished second in the voting for the first Kopa Trophy, an award given to the best player in Europe aged under 21.

He'd spent a year in England as a child, so Christian had seen the huge stadiums of Anfield, Old Trafford and Wembley.

English was still his native language and, although he was now a competent German speaker, he wasn't completely comfortable in everyday conversation.

So it was only natural that he was drawn to the Premier League.

At Dortmund, he'd played against English teams and he'd watched them on TV. He knew that the style was fast and relentless, with a lot of running and pressing.

It suited him down to the ground.

Dortmund had been trying to get him to sign a new

contract, but Christian didn't want to be tied down just yet. He wanted options.

"What do you think?" he asked his dad.

"Liverpool have Jürgen Klopp. You enjoyed working with him in the short time you were together at Dortmund, didn't you?"

Christian nodded, remembering Klopp's huge smile around the Dortmund training ground.

"They've also just reached the Champions League final," Mark added. "And they look like they might win the league this year."

"But their front three, with Salah, Mané and Firmino, isn't going to change," Christian sighed. "What about Arsenal?"

"Could be an opportunity to become a key part of the team rebuild, with Wenger gone," his dad suggested with a shrug.

"I've seen them play," Christian said. "Emery's style … " He paused, leaving it unsaid. They both knew that the slow style of play favoured by Unai Emery wouldn't suit Christian.

"So, what about Chelsea?" Christian sighed.

His dad's face lit up instantly. Christian had had a trial at Chelsea as a youngster. It had only been five days, but he'd seen the inside of the stadium, met the coaches and seen the training ground.

He knew his dad had been enthralled, but at the time it wasn't to be.

Perhaps this was fate. To end up back at that same club, to finish what he'd started there.

"They're the only ones who've actually been in touch," Mark reminded him. "They gave us a tour of the ground. They know Pennsylvania, they do a lot of charity work."

"But isn't that all for show?'" Christian countered. "They're just trying to get us onside."

"None of the other clubs have gone to those lengths though."

Christian couldn't disagree with that.

"Well, there's always a different country," Mark suggested. "La Liga, Serie A. Or you could stay at Dortmund. There's no need to rush into … "

"No," Christian interrupted. "I want to go to the Premier League." He paused for a second.

"Perhaps it *is* fate," he said, echoing his thoughts from earlier. "But would Dortmund accept a move?"

A few days later, Christian's agent phoned him.

"I've been talking to the directors at Dortmund – and they'll let you go. But they want 58 million pounds for you, which is about 73 million dollars."

"Woah!" Christian replied. That was crazy money, and it would make him one of the most expensive players in the world.

Surely, there was no way Chelsea were going to pay that.

"They've already met the asking price!" Christian's agent shouted excitedly down the phone. "Shows how much they think of you!"

"Seriously?" Christian replied in disbelief. He didn't know what to say.

"The deal includes a clause that you be loaned back to Dortmund for the rest of the season, because it'll be difficult to replace you in the January window," Christian's agent continued. "But, from July 1st, you're going to be a Premier League player. For one of the biggest clubs in the world."

It had been a while since the spotlight of the US media had been on Christian, but with this signing the focus on him would be sharper than ever.

Every eye was going to be on the most expensive American player in history.

Now all he had to do was deliver.

13
TURNING IT AROUND

July 2019, Nissan Stadium, Nashville, USA
Gold Cup Semi-Final, Jamaica v USA

"Most of us weren't here two years ago," Gregg Berhalter said, looking around at the players in front of him. "I wasn't here, Christian wasn't, Weston wasn't."

Berhalter was the fourth coach in charge of the US team since Christian had been given his debut. So far, Gregg was Christian's favourite.

"Two years ago, we won this tournament. We beat

Jamaica to win it. And today, we're playing them again," Gregg told the players.

He paused and looked directly at them, making sure he had their attention.

"Now, I know I don't need to tell you this. Nearly two years ago, we were beaten by Trinidad and Tobago. They were a team who were out for revenge. We thought that would be an easy game, a walk in the park – and it wasn't. They beat us."

He paused again, making sure he was getting his point across.

"Jamaica will be out for the same today. They will want revenge. For us, this game will *not* be a walk in the park. If we want to win it – we'll need to fight for it."

Then Christian spoke up. He was now one of the more experienced players in the squad – as well as being the most expensive American player of all time.

"We start fast, lads!" he said, clapping his hands together. "Don't give them a chance to think about revenge. We get the game done and we get ourselves in that final – against Mexico on Sunday!"

A few moments later, the teams were out on the

pitch, in front of a packed crowd of almost 30,000 fans. The game was being played in the USA, but Christian could still hear the huge Jamaican contingent who had made the trip.

As they lined up for the anthems, Christian thought back to the game against Trinidad and Tobago, and how he'd missed his chance to play at the World Cup as a result.

He'd been desperately disappointed that he hadn't been there. He wasn't going to let his country down again.

The US started strongly, with Jordan Morris and Reggie Cannon both having chances inside the first 10 minutes.

And then they broke the deadlock. Cannon volleyed the ball into the box and Weston McKennie burst in, taking a touch before firing past the keeper.

The USA had taken an early lead.

The sound inside the stadium went up a few decibels and now it was deafening. Christian could no longer hear the Jamaican fans.

A couple of minutes later, Christian almost doubled

the advantage when he rattled a free kick off the post. The US were dominating Jamaica and it looked to be only a matter of time before they got their second.

Then, astonishingly, an electrical storm swept its way over the stadium and, with the threat of lightning, the game had to be stopped until the storm had passed over.

For an hour and a half, the players sat huddled in their dressing rooms, waiting for the game to restart.

"We're playing really well, lads," Berhalter insisted. "Don't change a thing when we get back out there. Just keep doing what you're doing."

The enforced break wasn't good for either team, and when the match resumed it was slow to get going again.

Then, early in the second half, the USA struck. McKennie played a ball into Jordan Morris, who held off a challenge from a defender and got a shot away.

It was palmed out by the Jamaican keeper, but Christian was already there. He'd charged in, ahead of his marker and had got to the ball first.

He struck it with his right foot, crashing it into the back of the net.

GOAL!

Christian leapt into the air, fist-pumping the crowd.

But Jamaica weren't going to roll over and, a few minutes later, Shamar Nicholson got them a goal.

Now it was 2-1 to the USA.

The next 20 minutes were tense. The US team seemed to have forgotten how to attack, and they retreated further and further back, giving Jamaica plenty of room. A Jamaica goal seemed inevitable.

"We need to get forward," Christian muttered, seeing the direction the game was going.

Then he decided he'd have to do it himself.

He took the ball forward on the right, driving into the box and skipping past the defenders. He cut the ball back, looking for a run from midfield, but the ball eluded everyone and went to the far post.

It fell to Paul Arriola, who whipped a shot towards goal. Once more, it was saved by the Jamaican keeper, and once more it fell to the feet of Christian.

All he had to do was tap it past the keeper – already on the floor – into the back of the net.

With 5 minutes left, the USA were 3-1 up. The game was won.

"Don't get so excited yet, boys," Christian told his team-mates as they congratulated him on his brace. "We've got a final to win yet."

14

HAT-TRICK HERO

October 2019, Turf Moor, Burnley, England
Burnley v Chelsea

"Trust me, mate, there's no tougher place to play in the Premier League than Burnley on a cold Saturday evening," César Azpilicueta told Christian.

As Christian stood on the pitch, shivering in the chilly autumn air and waiting for the kick-off, he knew what the Chelsea captain meant.

He'd been "properly" at Chelsea for four months

now. In that time, they had appointed a new manager in Frank Lampard, had been hit by a transfer ban, lost a Super Cup final to Liverpool and been beaten 4-0 by Manchester Utd.

But more recently they had steadied the ship and had got themselves to fourth in the Premier League table.

It had been a whirlwind start to Christian's career in England. He'd started three of his first four games at the club, but he'd mostly been an unused substitute ever since.

"Costing 58 million doesn't guarantee you a place in the starting line-up at a club like Chelsea," Lampard told him. "We have a lot of special players and I always have to do what's right to get the win. But you're more direct than Eden Hazard, so when you're on the pitch, you'll need to make an impact and change games for us."

"Burnley's a long way from Hershey, right?" Mason Mount grinned, catching Christian looking around the stadium.

"We don't do grounds like this, back home," Christian answered. "Everything here is so old – it looks like it might fall down any minute."

"It probably might," Mount laughed. "And wait 'til they start singing and chanting and booing. They're so close to the pitch. Feels like they're right next to you."

"Anyway, it's the players that are more of a nightmare here," Tammy Abraham said. "They'll try and get in your face, wind you up."

"Oh yeah," Mount agreed.

"Trust me, that's nothing new," Christian scoffed.

The game started with plenty of Burnley pressure. They pumped long ball after long ball into the Chelsea box and the Burnley crowd were boisterous and rowdy.

After 10 minutes, the game slowed and Chelsea began to find their way into the game. Twenty minutes in, Matt Lowton took too long on the ball and Christian pounced, nipping the ball away from him and charging into open space.

The other defenders got across to cover, blocking Christian's run into the box, so he slowed down, threw a step over across the ball and knocked it onto his left foot. Wrapping his foot around the ball, he struck it hard. It spun through the crowd of players, past the keeper and into the back of the net.

GOAL! 1-0!

"Maybe Burnley's not so hard after all," Christian grinned.

It was his first Chelsea goal and it felt like a huge moment of release and relief. Now he'd got that landmark under his belt, he could play with a bit less pressure.

A few seconds before half-time, Christian struck again. Once more, he picked the ball up in Burnley's half and had space to drive into. This time, he got the ball onto his right foot, picked his spot and drove it low along the ground. It had too much pace for the keeper, beating him at the near post.

It was a crucial goal – for Christian and for Chelsea. 2-0! They were cruising.

"Left foot. Then right foot," Tammy Abraham grinned, embracing Christian. "So a header next – make it a perfect hat-trick!"

Christian nodded. He'd never scored a professional hat-trick, and this would be a great moment to do it. It would show that he could deliver, even in the tough games.

He wasn't sure he'd score a header though – that had never really been his style.

But then, just 10 minutes later, it became his style. A corner was cleared back to Mason Mount on the left-hand side. Christian was waiting in the box, ready for anything that might come his way.

The ball floated towards him and he rose, lifting his head and flicking the ball back into the danger zone. It didn't go quite where he'd intended, but instead floated into the far corner and into the net.

Chelsea were 3-0 up – and Christian had scored all three!

"There you go!" Mount shouted to him, as Christian held up three fingers to the travelling Chelsea fans behind the goal, who were all going wild. "A perfect hat-trick! Can't remember the last time we had one of them!"

Christian smiled and embraced his team-mates, looking around at the stadium that had seemed so menacing just an hour earlier. It had taken some time, but he felt at home in England now. He felt at home at Chelsea.

And he was just getting started.

15
BACK IN STYLE

June 2020, Stamford Bridge, London, England
Chelsea v Manchester City

"Is it tough, not being guaranteed a start each week?" Christian's dad asked him.

Before the pandemic lockdown, Christian had travelled back to the USA, to recover from an injury and to spend some time with his family.

Of all the clubs that had shown interest in his son, Mark had pushed for Chelsea, and Christian could sense his dad's nervousness. He didn't want to be the father who'd pushed his son into making a mistake.

"It's … different," Christian answered, trying to work out how to explain it. "I'm just another player in the squad at Chelsea – it's not like the national team."

"And you prefer that?"

"Sometimes, yeah," Christian confessed. "And the level is so high. There's some unbelievable players there – Kanté, Jorginho, Willian, Mason Mount. Playing with them is fun. You learn a lot."

"And what about Lampard?" Mark asked. "How's he as a manager?"

"Less tactical than the Dortmund guys," Christian said. "Much more motivational, hands-on stuff."

The Burnley hat-trick had seemed to kick-start Christian's Chelsea career, and he'd scored in each of his next two matches.

But it hadn't lasted long. As Christian was finding out, he couldn't assume anything at Chelsea. If you went through a poor patch of form, they didn't have time to let you ride it out and come back stronger.

That was it. You were dropped.

And that was exactly what had happened to him. The injury didn't help, ruling him out for over three months.

Then the season was halted by the coronavirus pandemic. Christian was probably the only player who was glad to see a halt like this – it gave him an opportunity to recover from his injury.

The season finally resumed in June, with Chelsea in the hunt for a top-four place. Liverpool were running with the title, and Christian felt a pang of jealousy, wondering if he should have signed to Liverpool instead of Chelsea.

He came back in top form, scoring a crucial equaliser in a 2-1 win over Villa.

The next game was Manchester City.

"We all know what happens," Lampard told them, looking around the dressing room. "We win this and Liverpool, not City, win the league."

Christian nodded. He knew exactly what a win for Chelsea tonight would mean for Liverpool.

"But I don't care about that," Lampard continued. "I only care about Chelsea. We are *so* close to securing

Champions League for next year. A win today is going to be crucial. It'll send out a message for next year – Chelsea are back."

It was very strange playing in a stadium without fans. Christian could hear every shout from every player, even if they were at the other end of the pitch. It had the feel of a training game.

City were a possession-based side and they kept the ball for the first 35 minutes, pinning Chelsea back.

Chelsea had to be ready to strike when their chance came – which eventually it did. A breakdown in communication between City players on the half-way line allowed Christian to nip in and take the ball.

He burst into the box, wrapped his foot round the ball, and slipped it past the keeper, into the far corner.

GOAL!

He turned to celebrate with the fans, before realising that there were none. The stadium was empty.

So he slid along the ground towards the TV cameras, punching the air.

"You might have just scored a title-winning goal!" Mason Mount laughed, grabbing him.

"Or the goal that gets us the Champions League," Christian reminded him.

City came roaring back in the second half, with De Bruyne firing them level.

Christian almost put Chelsea back in front when he rounded the keeper, but his shot was cleared off the line by Kyle Walker. Moments later, there was a scramble in the box and Fernandinho handled the ball to give Chelsea a penalty.

Willian stepped up and converted the penalty, giving Chelsea the win and handing Liverpool the title.

"I guess it's nice for you to secure the title for your old manager," Mason said to Christian, as they walked off the pitch.

"Yeah, but next time, I'm going to win the title for *us*."

16
COUNT ON ME

December 2020, Stamford Bridge, London, England
Chelsea v Leeds United

"You had a great first year with us, Chris," Frank Lampard told Christian in a pre-season meeting. "Eleven goals was your best season ever, right?"

"Yeah," Christian said slowly.

"The transfer ban last year meant we couldn't make any signings," Lampard continued. "But now the ban's been lifted, the club's going to be making a few signings. And some players we sign are going to be in your position."

Christian wasn't sure what to say. He'd had one of the best seasons of his career, but now Lampard was hinting that he might be replaced.

"Yeah," Christian said again.

This was what he'd been warned about during his time at Dortmund. You had to impress at the big clubs – or you got moved on.

After the Man City match, the goals and assists had kept coming for Christian, and he'd finished the season with 11 goals and 10 assists in all competitions, including a goal in the FA Cup final against Arsenal.

But that cup goal had been a bittersweet moment for Christian. He'd limped off later in the game and had been forced to watch as Arsenal came back and won the cup. Despite scoring in the final, Chelsea had finished the season trophyless.

Lampard's new signings soon arrived. Some of them, like Édouard Mendy, Thiago Silva and Ben Chilwell weren't going to impact Christian, but Kai Havertz, Timo Werner and Hakim Ziyech all would. These were all players who shared Christian's position in the attacking third of the pitch. Pedro and Willian had departed, but there were still the likes of Mason Mount, Callum Hudson-Odoi and Tammy Abraham.

Christian was going to have to fight for his place this year.

He missed six of the first nine games with a hamstring injury and wasn't used much from the bench when he was fit, with Lampard preferring the likes of Werner and Ziyech.

Chelsea's next game was at home against newly-promoted Leeds. A win would put Chelsea top of the table – at least for 24 hours, so there was a huge amount riding on it. It was also the first game with a limited number of fans – just 2,000 – allowed back in the stadium.

It wasn't many fans, but Christian could already sense a huge difference in the atmosphere. He'd got used to playing in empty stadiums, but hearing the roars and the chants of the crowd reminded him just how important they were. It made it a different game.

Christian started the game on the bench, but he

was brought on after 30 minutes to replace the injured Hakim Ziyech.

The game was already level at 1-1 when he came on, and it took a Kurt Zouma goal in the second half to get Chelsea in front.

But Leeds were pushing hard. Chelsea couldn't afford to drop points in the title race. They needed another goal to secure the win.

With just seconds left, Chelsea broke. Timo Werner burst away down the right-hand side and Christian sprinted forward through the middle, in support.

"Timo! Centre!" he roared, finding a burst of pace to get past the Leeds defender in front of him.

Timo fired the ball across the box and Christian got there first, sliding in to poke the ball into the back of the net.

"YES!" he shouted, embracing Timo as they celebrated together.

Christian hadn't just sent a message to the fans – he'd sent a message to the manager too. He wasn't going to give up his place in the Chelsea starting eleven without a fight.

17
UNDERDOGS

April 2021, Estadio Alfredo di Stefano, Madrid, Spain
Champions League Semi-Final First Leg, Real Madrid v Chelsea

"It's good to see a familiar face here," Thomas Tuchel told Christian. "You'll have to introduce me to everyone."

After a run of poor results that saw Chelsea slide down to ninth in the table, Frank Lampard was sacked. His replacement was a man that Christian was all too familiar with from his time at Dortmund. Thomas Tuchel.

Christian was glad to have a manager in charge that knew him, but at the same time he felt uneasy. At Dortmund, Tuchel had used him sparingly – mainly as an impact sub off the bench. That had been OK at the age of 17 or 18, but Christian was older now. He wanted to be playing from the start.

Tuchel quickly adapted Chelsea's style of play, moving to a more rigid 3-4-3. This had reduced the number of attacking spots available in the team. It put Christian in direct competition with the likes of Mason Mount, Tammy Abraham and Timo Werner. Before, there may have been room for all of them. Now there wasn't.

"Maybe you could retrain as a wing-back to increase your chance of getting into the team," Christian's dad had suggested, the last time they'd spoken on the phone.

"That might have worked at Dortmund, but I'm in a different situation now," Christian had replied. He'd cost Chelsea almost £60 million, he'd scored in the FA Cup final and he'd captained his country. He wanted to play in the front three – and he knew he was good enough to do it.

"Well ... as much as I wanted you to join Chelsea,

that doesn't mean you have to stay forever," his dad had pointed out. "You can work hard and impress Tuchel all you like, but if your playing time is limited, stopping you from becoming the best player you can be, that's the time to move on."

Christian had been so caught up in playing for Chelsea that he hadn't really considered moving away. Plenty of teams had been interested in him when he'd joined Dortmund and Chelsea, and he knew there'd be potential suitors now.

"I don't want to give up so easily," he told his dad. "I've got the number 10 shirt and I'm not going to stop working until I become a Chelsea legend in it."

So, under Tuchel, Christian worked hard and tried to make the most of his cameos off the bench.

He scored against West Brom, got an assist against Burnley, and then scored a brace against Palace. His cameo appearances gradually got longer, and slowly they were being turned into starts.

It had become clear that Tuchel was a step up from Lampard. Christian noticed that everything the manager was doing, from tactics to match preparation, was decided right down to the little details. He was clever, meticulous and highly organised.

And it was working.

Chelsea had rocketed up the table and were now back in the running for a Champions League spot. Plus, they were through to the final of the FA Cup and were in the semi-finals of the Champions League, where their opponents were the most successful team in the competition – Real Madrid.

Christian had played against Real Madrid when he'd been with Dortmund. Thanks to players like Karim Benzema, Sergio Ramos, Toni Kroos and Luka Modrić, Real had won the Champions League four times in the past seven years. Beating them would be making a sensational statement.

Owing to COVID, the first leg was held in Real Madrid's training ground stadium. It didn't have the same atmosphere as the immense Santiago Bernabéu Stadium that Real Madrid were renowned for, but even so, watching the Real players warm up sent a shiver down Christian's spine.

"We can't be scared of them," Tuchel warned before

the game. "Don't show them too much respect. If you give Kroos and Modric' time on the ball, they will kill us."

"They're Real Madrid, but they're still human," the captain César Azpilicueta added. "It's still eleven versus eleven out there on that pitch."

"A good result here and we can take them on back at the Bridge," Tuchel continued. "We don't need to win. Just stay compact, work hard. We will get chances. We just have to take them."

Christian's recent run of form had earned him a spot in the starting line-up, starting in the front three alongside Mason Mount and Timo Werner.

Christian glanced over at the Real Madrid bench as they came out the tunnel, spotting the familiar shape of their manager Zinedine Zidane next to them. Zidane was somebody that Christian had idolised as a kid.

Looking across at the faces of the Chelsea players, Christian could see their steely determination. Chelsea might be the underdogs, but the players all knew that they were capable of winning this.

The game started well for Chelsea. Christian and

Mason were finding all sorts of spaces and gaps, and they were causing problems for the Madrid midfield.

Chelsea got their first chance inside 10 minutes. Mount's curled shot looped up in the air, coming towards Christian. He headed it back across goal to Werner, but his strike was straight at the keeper.

Christian put his hands to his head. He couldn't believe Chelsea weren't in front. He knew how important it was for them to take their chances – and that had been one of the biggest.

A few minutes later, just 15 minutes into the game, Antonio Rüdiger floated a ball over the defence to Christian, who'd made a darting run across the box. Christian wasn't sure if he was onside, but out of the corner of his eye he saw the linesman's flag stay down.

Controlling the ball, he turned and faced down the huge figure of Thibaut Courtois in the Real Madrid goal. Christian used his agility to dribble round the Belgian keeper as he fell to the ground.

The Real Madrid defenders were now backed up on the goal-line, but Christian took a breath and slammed the ball with the inside of his boot. It flew through the air and went between all of them, smashing into the back of the net.

GOAL!

Chelsea were ahead, away to Real Madrid!

Christian wasn't concerned about the VAR check. He knew he was onside, he knew he'd timed his run.

He turned and sprinted over to the Chelsea bench, embracing his team-mates and coaches, the people who had believed in him over the last few months. Everyone involved in the team knew how important his goal could be, in their bid to win the best club competition in the world.

But Madrid's formidable reputation wasn't for nothing. Benzema went close a few minutes later, and then shortly after that he volleyed in an equaliser.

Now it was 1-1.

The game continued at the same breakneck pace and Christian was involved multiple times, fizzing balls across the box and creating chances for team-mates.

Exhausted, he was subbed off after 65 minutes, but he didn't feel disappointed. He'd given everything for his team and had scored a crucial goal in a Champions

League semi-final. It didn't get much better than that.

Chelsea managed to hold on for the 1-1 draw, a huge result that put them in the driving seat for the second leg.

"I can't wait to get back to the Bridge," Christian said to Mason in the dressing room, as they took off their boots. "We'll bury them once and for all."

18
STRONGER THAN EVER

January 2022, Stamford Bridge, London, England

Chelsea v Liverpool

"Every day people come up to me in the street, asking how you're getting on," Mark told his son. "Even over here, winning the Champions League like that got you a lot of extra fans! People keep telling me you're a legend, one of the greats."

"Dad, I'm 22!" Christian told him. "Don't call me a legend yet! It makes it sound like my career's already over."

Chelsea had beaten Real Madrid 2-0 in the second leg, winning 3-1 on aggregate. Christian had been at the centre of it once again, setting up Mason Mount to secure the win.

He was then a substitute in the final, as Chelsea beat Premier League rivals – and favourites for the trophy – Man City, 1-0.

Chelsea had become Champions of Europe for the second time – Christian for his first. He became the first American to play in a Champions League final, and just the second American to win the competition.

The summer brought just one incoming signing for Chelsea – striker Romelu Lukaku, as Tuchel strengthened his forward line. Christian had been in and out of the team in the previous season, but he hoped his strong finish to the campaign would give the boss more reason to play him.

With capacity crowds back in stadiums at the beginning of the new season, there was a new level of expectation at the club.

"How do they expect us to top winning the Champions League?" Christian asked Timo Werner.

As a good German speaker, Christian got on well with the German internationals Timo, Kai Havertz and Antonio Rüdiger.

"I don't think they expect us to win the Champions League again," Timo replied. "Only Real Madrid have ever won it back-to-back. But we do need to be competing in multiple competitions – and playing at a similar level to last season. And to do that, we're going to need squad depth."

The season started well. It had been a long time since Christian had played in front of full crowds, and he quickly found his feet, scoring on the opening day in a win against Crystal Palace.

Then, just days later, disaster struck. Christian picked up coronavirus and was quarantined for a few weeks. When he did return, he picked up an ankle injury and didn't get to play again until November.

In his absence, Chelsea flourished. Lukaku was scoring goals and Kai Havertz was finding form.

Ziyech, Mount, Werner and Hudson-Odoi had all moved past him in the pecking order.

On top of that, Ross Barkley and Ruben Loftus-Cheek

had both returned from loan moves and were fighting for their own places in the squad.

Christian's year had just got a whole lot harder.

It took him a while to force his way back into the team. Although the competition to get a start in a game was fiercer than it had been, the good news was that Chelsea were fighting on multiple fronts. All the players were getting a lot of game time.

They sealed their first trophies of the year in the European Super Cup and the Club World Cup. On top of that, they were still in the Champions League, the FA Cup and the League Cup, and were well within the top three in the Premier League.

"How many trophies do you think we're gonna win?" Christian asked Jorginho, after one training session.

"Don't get ahead of yourself, mate," the experienced Italian midfielder replied. "Let's just take things one game at a time. We need to beat Liverpool on Sunday if we want a chance at winning the league."

Chelsea might be champions of Europe, but they hadn't been champions of England for almost five years.

The Liverpool game was critical. Managed by

Christian's first coach at Dortmund, Jürgen Klopp, Liverpool were brilliant – ruthless and hard-working. They were not an easy side to beat.

The media were also describing the game as a battle between Tuchel and Klopp, a match-up between Christian's two former Dortmund bosses.

With the team's strikers, Lukaku and Werner, both out injured, Christian found himself lining up as the side's main striker.

"You three need to keep rotating positions and confuse the defenders, just like you did in the game at Real Madrid," Tuchel told Christian, Mason Mount and Kai Havertz before kick-off.

"We know what's up for grabs today, boys," Tuchel announced before the game. "The Premier League title."

He paused, letting the words sink in.

"We've slipped behind," he continued. "We can point the finger at injuries, at the schedule, bad luck … whatever you want to call it. But we're behind."

He looked round the room, sizing them up, seeing which players were up to the challenge.

"But it's early. We win today, we fight today, then

we send out a message. 'Chelsea are going for the title. Chelsea are back.'"

Christian had heard the same sentiments before. Frank Lampard had said similar things. But, coming from Tuchel, it seemed to carry more weight. It seemed more believable. It felt as if Chelsea really *were* back.

Very early in the game, Christian almost scored. The ball fell to him on the edge of the box but, instead of shooting first time, he attempted to dribble around the keeper. A huge, gloved hand from Caoimhin Kelleher stopped him and the chance disappeared.

Christian cursed under his breath. That was a chance and he should have taken it. Against Liverpool, chances like that would be few and far between.

A moment later, he felt even worse about his miss, when Sadio Mané gave Liverpool the lead, before Mo Salah flicked the ball over Mendy to make it 2-0.

Chelsea now had a mountain to climb, against one of the best teams in the world.

Looking around at his fellow players, Christian felt a sense of responsibility. This was just like his time with the national team. He had to step up.

He began pulling the team forward and, just before half-time, Mateo Kovačić pulled a goal back, volleying in from outside the box.

As the second half began, it felt as if the momentum was now with Chelsea. Liverpool had their backs to the wall, defending their lead.

Antonio Rüdiger won the ball, feeding N'Golo Kanté in midfield. Before the ball had even reached the Frenchman's feet, Christian was already making his run in behind.

Kante flicked the ball over the head of the defender and it bounced in front of Christian. Controlling it in his stride, he just had the keeper to beat.

With his left foot, he directed a powerful left-footed volley towards the top-right corner.

GOAL!

Chelsea were level.

Christian kissed the Chelsea badge on his shirt as he roared towards the stands. It was an overwhelming feeling to have the fans cheering his name again.

With the game running out a 2-2 draw, there was now no doubt. Chelsea were most definitely back.

19

FROM PENNSYLVANIA TO QATAR

March 2022, Exploria Stadium, Orlando, Florida, USA
World Cup Qualifiers, USA v Panama

"You're the captain, Chris. Say a few words." Gregg Berhalter, the USA manager, turned to Christian, inviting him up to give his team-mates some encouragement.

Captain America glanced around the dressing room. It was the eighth time he'd worn the captain's armband.

This moment counted. The USA were playing Panama, and a win would qualify the USA for the

2022 World Cup in Qatar. Even if they lost, they'd still probably qualify, but Christian hadn't forgotten a similar situation five years ago, when a defeat against Trinidad had knocked them out.

Nothing less than a win here would do.

"Let's punch our ticket to the World Cup," Christian said, before sitting down again. He didn't need to say anything else. His team-mates knew what was on the line. They knew what they had to do.

Christian wasn't going to miss out on another opportunity to play at the World Cup finals. He was now the main man for his country, the pressure mostly falling on his shoulders. For a long time it had felt uncomfortable, but now he relished it.

There was a packed crowd in the stadium, all ready to watch the US make up for that loss five years ago.

After just 14 minutes, the USA got their moment. A scrap in the Panama box resulted in a VAR check, which awarded the USA a penalty.

Christian was the captain, he was their penalty taker. This was his moment.

"Where am I putting it?" he asked Tyler Adams.

"Top bins," Adams replied.

Christian nodded and turned to face down the keeper. He'd been half-joking when he'd spoken to his team-mate, but now, looking at the keeper, he realised it was good advice.

He breathed out slowly, looking at the crowd. All eyes were on him.

He charged forward and lashed the ball high into the top corner of the net.

1-0.

Any nerves that the team had felt earlier were suddenly put to bed. Now they had the advantage. They already had one foot in the World Cup finals.

A few minutes later, Paul Arriola doubled their lead, and then Jesus Ferreira added a third.

Then, moments before half-time, the USA got another penalty. Christian was once more the man standing in front of the keeper.

This time, he didn't need any help from a team-mate. He charged forward and blasted the ball hard. The keeper went the right way, but his dive was too short. Christian was on a hat-trick and the USA were four up. Suddenly it looked as if the World Cup party had started early in the Exploria Stadium.

Christian's third goal seemed inevitable. Just after the hour mark, the ball was crossed in from the left wing and Christian controlled it with his left foot, while spinning away from his defender.

He knocked the ball past another defender with his next touch and placed it into the bottom right corner with his right foot.

GOAL!

It was his best goal of the lot and it completed his first international hat-trick. It was also a goal that effectively secured an American presence at the World Cup finals.

Christian jogged away calmly, basking in the cheers of the US fans. They'd come to see their star player – and he'd delivered.

This is what dreams are made of, he thought.

A few minutes later, he was subbed off and, as he walked off the pitch, he savoured the standing ovation that the American crowd were giving him.

He was the man who had led his nation to a World

Cup. He was the most expensive American player in history, a Champions League winner, a Club World Cup winner … he had already won so much in his career.

These were achievements that many players would be happy with, looking back at the end of their careers.

But Christian was still only 23 years old.

He looked around at the crowd once more. In nine months' time, these fans would be supporting him at a World Cup.

But, before travelling to Qatar, he had time to win even more trophies with Chelsea, and to establish himself as one of the best players in the world.

Then there would be the 2026 World Cup, in North America. By then, Christian would be 27 years old, close to the pinnacle of his career.

He had opportunities to make history – in Qatar, in the USA in 2026, and at club level. He was going to cement his place as the greatest American footballer ever.

He was Christian Pulisic, and he wasn't going to let it slip.

HOW MANY
HAVE YOU READ?

MESSI · KANE · RONALDO · HAALAND · SALAH

PULISIC · LEWANDOWSKI · RASHFORD · MBAPPÉ · SON

KANTÉ · VAN DIJK · NEYMAR